SOULS
UNRAVEL

Michelle L. Tate

To Deb,
Thank you for your friendship.
My heart appreciates it.
Love to You,
Michelle

Somewhere
between here and there,
yesterday and tomorrow,
intention and action,
thought and confusion,
one moment and eternity.

External shell is
beginning to show signs
of the battle,
of the fatigue,
of the see-saw between
everywhere and nowhere.

My soul shifts.
Not fast, not slow.

....unraveling?   Is that what I just heard?

Feels like a separating of something that is trying to stay close.

These eyes have grown blurry and blood-shot red.
Nowhere is okay with that.

Some old and new injuries show no signs of surrender.
Why are they calling my name?

In the coming apart, I feel it.
Something is about to give.

NOT nowhere.
RIGHT here.

Souls move.
Not always fast or slow.
Sometimes, they are simply unraveling...
bidding us to explore not only the outside, but also the "in."

CONTENTS

ACKNOWLEDGMENTS

To my friends who are soul searching, and to those whose souls are searching. It is our shared journey.

Without support, encouragement, belief and love from any and all of you, perhaps some loneliness would own much of my every moment.

Deeply, I thank you.

To my family. Core gratitude and love at the deepest level. Inspirations and despairs are shared among us, leaving us each where we stand today. Sometimes close in proximity, sometimes not. Anyway, love travels all time and distance. Always and no matter what, I love you.

To my Mom. The guard, the keeper, the treasure, the angel. I have no idea how she does it, but she keeps doing it. I love you Mom. Thank you for teaching me about life and depth - about having courage to find things that matter to my soul, and about trying to do a little something about it.

PROTECTOR

What happens in our world
breaks my heart about a million times a day.
The other times, I close my eyes and
say I do not see.
For each of these times,
my heart inherits a scar.

Soul's journey takes her twists and turns. I have found no
bumpers to ease the hard knocks and crashes.

Soul grows up, falls down, gets worn, starts to unravel,
dropping us into our own lessons, dares and truths.

What's in there?

I once imagined myself to be a protector.

I have failed - from the very beginning and into today.

I could not protect
the woman who gave me life.

Not from heartache, worry, sadness,
fear, pain, broken bones, divorce,
cancer.   me.

How can I make myself "fit" to be alive?

Some have told me that I have a gift.
Some ability to realize the connectedness
of us and all things.

Is it?

What is the gift of feeling
your anger, *your* fright and worst nightmares?
Or in touching *your* injury
and feeling it burn its way through
my body....?

What kind of gift have I been given?
How do I appreciate it?

What happens in our world
breaks my heart about a million times a day.

The other times, I close my eyes and
say I do not see.
For each of these times,
my heart inherits a scar.

A scarred liver can kill you.
I imagine the same is so of a heart.

I am no protector.
I have protected no body, no soul,
not even my own.

….but somewhere, deep inside,
is a voice reminding me that I have also
not protected anyone from such things as
love, joy, pleasure, happiness, peace….

And so, how then dare I call myself "failure?"

There is this light in me…I know.

Worn only with love,
it will never grow dim – even for myself.

Perhaps I'd be wise to try and protect only that.

COST OF COMFORT

Without a comfort zone
there comes an edge
that can't be drawn
and barely seen
but rather keenly
felt.

Considering comfort.

Try

    To

        NOT

           Find

              It.

Or, find it only

        slightly

          over-rated.

In comfort,

one expects he or she knows

just what there is to know.

Some expectation gets built in the mind.

So,
can you throw it away?

Live there?

Without a comfort zone
　　there comes an edge
　　　　that can't be drawn
　　　　and barely seen
　　　　　　but rather keenly
　　　　　　felt.

Uncertainty.

'Don't know' what's next.

Uncover some comfort in that.

In this place, you are free to experience

　　the instant of some happening

　　　　instead of being stuck on what you

　　　　　thought

　　was　going　to　happen.

Anyone ever tell you that

it's okay to go

　　outside the lines?

~ This can be a place where magnificently

    terrifying

        beautifully

            heart-breaking

      lessons

   show up

to meet

    and touch

      and grow

           your soul. ~

Not feeling at home anywhere

isn't always a sad or bad thing.

It *can* be about *possibility*.

Well anyway,

I don't always have to know what's next.

In fact, I never truly do.

I think
it's just someplace

we sometimes

    Try
        To
            Run
                From.

Today?

finds

me

just

sitting

right

here...

letting old robber
    comfort
        run off with the wind.

FEAR CAGE

An earthly sensation.
Seems real enough,
especially when it locks us down.

FEAR

An earthly sensation.

Seems real enough,

      especially when it locks us down.

Yet, your spirit desires freedom.

   In fact,

intimately *knows* freedom

   and truth

     and light.

Earth experience helps
us to grow this cage
called
    FEAR.

Of the things we grow well
on this plane,
this is one of our
great successes.

We grow it amazingly strong.

Exceptionally well-built.

Masterfully even.

By the time we've reached <u>any</u> older age,

we are old enough to know

that we *used to know*

something different before.

By then
we are looking to the outside

from behind
our once upon a time
foreign feeling
vision blocking

hindering

bars.

Seems we are willing
to take advice
regarding
this contraption
surrounding us.

Seems we take the most advice
concerning ways
to protect
and keep
us safe;

11

encouraging us to toughen,
    reinforce and accelerate
        the growing of
            our home-made barriers...

so.

Can I offer some advice?

Come closer.

I'll just push up against your chilly bars
    and whisper to any soul
        still listening...

These bars?

My friend,

I can recommend only this.

        BREAK THEM.

Don't worry.
Or do.

Words, even on a whisper,
can sometimes reach
inside the cage,

on some level can be heard...

        break them.

2,000-YEAR-OLD COUGH

I have this 2,000-year-old cough
telling me that I'm dead.
I have a pain in my chest
telling me that I'm not.

I have this 2,000-year-old cough
telling me that I'm dead.

I have a pain in my chest
telling me that I'm not.

I have stood completely alone before.

I liked it then.

The loneliness consuming me now
is different.

I don't like it, but
I'm trying not to dislike it either.

I tell myself it's good.
or not.
or whatever.

or that it is here and soon it will go.

I close my eyes and tell myself
of the love I have for me,

and that others love me too.

Tell myself I'm worth it.

And here,

again,

I fall apart.

Too alone to appreciate
the coming and going just yet,

and this cough won't let me
breathe anyway.

Working on the
come and go,

but I can't get out of this
shattered body
that's trying so hard
to kill me.

I am freshly reminded that

if I can't figure out

how to love me

as I love all around me,

this "it" will succeed

and in my next life,

I'll be choking on a
2,001 year old death...

CREATE

It can only come
if I go
It can only be so
If I say so

It can only come
if I go

It can only be so
If I say so

I'm getting bored with
this dying routine.

I mean, how many
ways can it change?

It's all the same in the end.

Want to
Line
Back
up.

Small voice heard.

Just get going.

We'll be back
        for you later
                or later
                        or later

or not.

What did I miss?

Feel a shift coming on.

Shifting from,
"What's happening to me?"

to - "Remember what happened last time?"

to - "How far are you going to take me this go 'round?"

to - "Give me some detail before we head out,
maybe it's nowhere I want to go again..."

They laugh.
Me too.

They laugh at me while I don't cry.
Me too.

They cry.
I do not.

I hear music and a chant
on the breeze.

"loveandloveandloveandlove
andloveandpeaceandpeaceand
piecetogetherloveandpeaceand
lovetogetherpiecedtogetherpeacedtogetherlove"

It doesn't stop.
It never stops.

Oh...so *that's* why I'm still here.

DESERT WITH BUDDHA

"What is your question?"

My throat cracked,
Filled with sand,
No voice poured out.

In the desert,
I sat with Buddha.

One hour,
        Eight,

        27 days,

                49 months,

                    852 years,

                        And 16 minutes...

"What is your question?"

My throat cracked,
Filled with sand,
No voice poured out.

"The silence has your answer."

Then I was born to noise.

                .....i miss sitting in the desert with Buddha....

ACT OF MY OWN

What is that?
Is there really such a thing,
in this world we share?

I have had things and lost them.

Some by my own hand,
some through no act of my own.

"Act of my own."

What is that?

Is there really such a thing,
      in this world we share?

I realize a new depth of gratitude today.

I have been given,
so that I might *experience*.

Have been stripped for reasons the same.

Not much found here
to invest in the chase
      for the victim,
            the blame,
                  or self-pity.

I know how it feels to have had
                              and then lost.

And who alive,
does not know this feeling?

This "something"
that's become somewhat known

moves with me now
        as I do the same
                through nights and days

                and nights again.

"True gift" of life?

                Of *my* life?

I give away so that I can remember
what it is to be without.

If attached, separate.
If stuck, let go.
If afraid, jump.

Hear the voice of a mystic friend named

        LIFE.

"I am here. Share with me your voice.
I am your greatest teacher.
I...am...*experience*."

FELL THROUGH THE SKY

I took off at a trot, which soon became running,
before I knew it,
I was flying.

Once had the keys,
I gave them away,

wondered later how I got here anyway.

They said, see that hole?
There's no way through.

But once I got on the other side,
they still wouldn't come on.

Stood back and said no,
saw no way to go,

      we just didn't fit,

            said I was wrong for doing it.

The Ones who I met, who helped me along

Yes, those Ones who helped me learn to be strong,
     became louder inside
         called me out for a ride.

After some hills a few twists and wide turns,
they gathered me up and sent me along,

     time to be on my way,

walk, don't run – advice they were selling.

So I took off at a trot, which soon became running,
     before I knew it,
          I was flying.

I met a bird who gave me a coin
I tried to go back and give them half
but they said it was useless and not even real

So I threw it in the ocean and met my first wave
who said, "Come on in and meet me my friend."

They said, "be careful, don't go too deep,"

and I ran to the rocks and jumped in with both feet

first meeting the wave who tore my body apart

I couldn't gain balance,

     couldn't feel where to start

          to find my way in the muck and the gray

clenched my teeth and rode through it

and my thoughts became still

     thought I was dead there,
     but it didn't end there,

wave gently lifted me to the rock in the sun
and my aching body, sprawled out to dry

too tired then even to cry

and I loved the ocean, and I loved the trees,
and I loved the mountains and the breeze
and I became very big with these thoughts and this love
and I shed my old skin and followed

the

young boy

who showed me the

stairs
       made
              of
                    stars.

His eyes were glowing with love and desire,
mischief even?

Made me go higher

until he lost me and I looked around
not even a sound

only cold darkness

    but it wasn't stillness,

there were stars throbbing and musing,
and I was amazed and in love.

And some Ones saw and called to me,

"Come home,
        come home,

                you used to be one of us."

My heart broke in two
and I fell through the sky

curled up like a fetus, I laid in a hole,
wrapped in water I didn't quite know.

Afraid to look up, afraid to look down,
I closed my eyes and stayed curled in that ball
of newborn vision, grateful and raw.

"Open your eyes now," I heard.

Heart beating fast,
I opened them to see

        the leaf of a flower towering above me

and the giant ant stood
like a dinosaur over my head,

and I loved him and the flower
as though they'd given me life,

and their beauty made me want to
crawl right out of my skin.

"Stand up now," I heard.

Trembling bones,
unfamiliar to me,

I stretched my limbs and I could see
that the water was a raindrop,

and I lived in a puddle
and I loved that raindrop like she was my mother
and I stood bare naked and lowered my head and wept
like the newborn baby I was.

"This is how I love you," I heard.

And I just couldn't bear it,
and I fell to my knees, so touched
by the power of this simplicity

and I couldn't get up, with my face covered up,
couldn't look up, not worthy of this,
I dug and dug,
trying to crawl back in.

"You are worth it," I heard. "Love *you*."

What did that mean? I rose up again, thin, raw skin,
looking around, beauty burning my eyes,
regarded the flower that once was my tower and
the ant that was my giant

took a rest on my sneaker,
and I offered my finger, helping him to
a new castle made of long grass.

And the raindrop that born me,
I wore on my glasses and it somehow changed my vision,

      everything different from here.

Scanning the blue sky,
beyond it the black sky,
beyond it eternity

      which appeared
         colorfully colorless.

...and the stars hugged me from there and
I shook where I stood,

     again broken-hearted,

       going down on one knee.

"Stand up," I heard. "Love *You*."

Someone threw me the keys to this castle I drive.

               Think I might keep 'em this time.

BORROWED STRENGTH

I will go through the fire to keep you well.
No monster could stop me, nothing could touch me.

...All is well...

Young eyes taking in the sights of struggle

I ran through the forest with borrowed strength
from the mountain,

catching her as she fell, too weary to walk.

"You are so strong," she said, "you are a young warrior."

I closed my eyes and gave her the mountain,
she rose and walked away.

Alone, I jumped so that he wouldn't have to.
I swam so that he could stay dry.
I read, so that you could listen to the words.
I built it, to protect you from the wind.

I will go through the fire to keep you well.

No monster could stop me, nothing could touch me.

All is well.

...there was a cry for help...

Looking around, nothing to see,
I heard it again.

A being cloaked in velvety orange
came through the wall before me.

Larger than my eyes could see,

he spoke without voice.

"Your *Self* needs you."

No breath came as these words sank in.

He moved closer.

I froze,
unable to move even one muscle.

"Your *Self* needs you."

I heard it in my soul
ripping apart from the inside out,

this arrow pierced through my heart like a bullet.

Falling to my knees and clutching at the gaping hole that
once was my heart,
my fingers searched for the strands that
might take it back.

The mountains who once fed me turned away.
The breeze wouldn't exhale to feed me my next breath.
The river stopped movement, nothing to match.

All around me stood beings
filled with colors
and not solid

not a single one moved.

Laying on my back on the place I would die,

I looked up into the sky
where the sun continued to shine all around me
but no longer on me.

Closed my eyes and waited for my end.

Then a being of Light came and stood above me,
laughing at my state.

Squinting under the light he cast, I tried to turn away.

Body wouldn't move and he continued to mock my
paralysis.

He leaned over me and placed his hand on the hole
where my heart
used to live.

Fire burned through my body and into my back,
melting me into a heap of useless flesh.

"Breathe," came the instruction.

Without question I inhaled the light and force he shared.

He backed away and I looked down,
my heart was there but not complete.

I sat up slowly, he stood before me,

    offering his hand of glowing movement.

Taking it, I rose then to my own shaky feet.

"Just breathe."

Again I took a breath, fed to me from universe,
beginning then to re-layer my heart and her home.

His eyes flashed with something I couldn't be sure of and
he invited the being cloaked in orange
to come forward again.

This presence alone set fire to my eyes.
Heart remembered the arrow quite well.

"Someone needs you," he said, coming closer.

"Well who is it? I am happy to go…"

He pointed then to my thin-skinned chest
and I crumbled in the place where I had
been trying to stand.

No breath would come and my throat closed up tight.
Again I fought for some vision, some sight
that would help me hold on, or help me stand up
instead there was silence and I felt completely alone,
except for the challenge to

     help

        "me."

The being of light spoke next.

"It's okay to die if you choose,
but you know you to be much stronger than that."

So I buckled in and entered the ride of my life,

    inward but outward,

        circling but sliding,

            reaching up but falling back

until I wound up

    in the silence of

        everywhere.

There,
in the center of my being,

in the center of the world,

I waited for the way to learn to love.

A little girl sat, with a book in her lap,
light blue pants, striped sweater,
braided sandy blonde hair, black shoes, white socks.

She was looking down, not up.

As I approached her
she continued to read,
her little feet rocking to
some music she heard.

"What are you doing?" I asked.

She looked up at me, eyes as big as the sea,
content, not unhappy at all.

"Reading."

I knelt down before her and she reached forward,
touching my face with
her tiny fingers, love-filled.

"How old are you?" I asked.
"Four."
"Wow. You can read and you're only 4?"

"My mom says that's how smart I am," she beamed.
    Her little feet kicked with excitement.

"Well do you know how special you are?" I asked.

Her eyes scrunched up, along with her nose.

She said, "My mom thinks I'm the best, smartest little girl
in the world."

"...but do you know how precious you are?" I asked.

She looked down at the book in her lap.

Feet stopped moving, hands folded on the page,
silent and still.

"Is it okay if I give you a hug?" I asked.

Shrugging her shoulders, she offered no "yes" and no
"no."

So my heart wrapped around her and I held her in my
arms and said to her,

"You are precious and I love you."

Her child-heart beat against mine, her mighty arms held
me ever so tight.

"Even if I couldn't read yet?" she asked in a whisper.

"Even if you could not read yet,
I love you and you are precious to me."

And she smiled into my soul and clung to me once more
and as I held her close,
        she dissolved into me,

                and I was left in tears,

sitting on the floor
of my soul.

I rocked back and forth for the longest time,
crying, dreaming, waiting for her to come back
so I could tell her something more.

But somehow I realized that she'd made it to the stars by
now - it was time for me to make my return.

So I ventured back up,
or out or around,

whichever the way
lacked any direction

but I woke up inside me,

to a flame burning before me,

to the scent of incense tickling my nose.

The one cloaked in orange bowed and faded off.

The being of Light touched my heart one more time,
advising.

"You must never turn your back
on the calling of your Self,

        or surely

                some part of you
                        will die.

So from now until forever,

wiser to remember...

all love

includes

your Self."

IF I ASKED YOU

Guess I didn't ask you
'cuz I didn't want to know
what would happen to this fire
if I didn't let it go.

Guess I didn't ask you
'cuz I didn't want to know
what would happen to this fire
if I didn't let it go.

Would it torch my inner lining
like that rocket
in the sky ?

Would it rip apart my organs
like that blast that
just went by?

I feel the outside, outside
and I feel the inside in,
but then they flip and flop around
condition changes then.

This vision becomes taste,
my taste buds offer sound,
my ears become more vocal
as I fight to stay on ground.

The earth becomes an ocean,
the walls begin to melt...

I wonder if I asked you,

would you have ever felt -
this craziness, unsettling,
frustration and this dream,
this rock and this cool water
and this steaming mountain spring.

This after hours visit
to this often lonely room
leaves me closed up like a flower
who has missed her time to bloom.

INJURY TEACHING ME

Injury is teaching me,
all the things I cannot be
Injury is teaching me,
all that I am free to be

Waiting for the words
to fall
once they rushed
but now they crawl

peaceful me to make
this so?

wonder now where did
they go...

racing through from
every angle
knotted up in
whirling tangles

quiet only outside
then,
wearing noise within,
                    within.

today.
sunlight warms the back of me,
creates the shadow I now see
slowing down inside of me
warming every part of me.

peacefully, so peacefully.

used to be sleep ran from me
close my eyes, now free to me

peacefully, so peacefully.

Injury is teaching me,
    all the things I cannot be

Injury is teaching me,
    all that I am free to be

becoming more a memory
    no longer such a part of me

program running
tried to blind me

no ability for softness,
hard I was inside and out,

it's what they thought I was about

my job was to take it.

to make it right
I tried to fake it

some believed their eyes
that
"saw" me

truth be told, they could *not* see

that I was not
who they had been

that I did wear a
thinner skin

that my heart broke
most every day

100 million different ways

yet did not leave me hard or mad
didn't need a good or bad
didn't build a wrong or right
didn't even close my eyes
rather took it all inside
turned me out, no place to hide

eyes bone dry...
can't even cry.

a little gift my dad gave me
tears inside, but none to see
can't afford to cry out loud
nothing to do with being proud
more to do with what I'd earned
tiny baby harshly learned
that tears would only hurt another
even tiny baby's mother
no more tears, they ended there
not because I didn't care

but more because I did.

my quiet was not confidence

that's what they thought they saw

my quiet was humility
a constant state of awe

break me down, get through my walls
no hands to catch my many falls
let me crumble, fill with doubt
and this is what it was about

watch me stumble, have me crawl
a steady state of soul withdrawal

make it so I thought I needed
every lesson, hard knocks heeded

loved me best when I was broken
came to me when I was choking
loved me when I died inside
pushed so hard to make me cry

told me I was hiding from
all the things I'd left undone
said that I was on the run
said that there was only one
to help me find a truer way

to help me greet a brighter day

guide my step and make me whole
and so we each assumed our role

and I became a shell of me
and lost
became the whole of me

walked the walls and halls of me
until I could no longer see

where I once stood or where it was
there was no me, there was now us

and they, the bigger party

I followed loss to the end of me,
trusted this to set me free

and in some way, it did.

free of knowing my own feeling
free of owning my own healing
free of all I'd come to be
free of even knowing me...

no longer even cared to.

rebuilding me became the task
I did as told, no questions asked

giving up the rooms of me
I let it in to live rent-free
a game I could not recommend
rules I could not comprehend
the promise of a better feeling
left me twisted up and reeling
something wasn't fitting right
tossed and turned most every night
inside of me felt torn apart
a constant aching in my heart

and finally, stepped back.

in the pause I met another
way to build a spirit

watching with full interest
and no longer did I fear it

opening, these openings
natural and flowing
feelings, such good feelings
began and just kept going
touching parts I'd put away
saying things I'd never say
a willingness to open up
there was no need to tear me up
capable of moving here
motivated not by fear

quite opposite, by trust.

revisit it. hurts less today.
can see it in a different way
no wrong, no right

        just part of me

moving now toward memory

Injury, is teaching me
        how *not* to be
            and how *to* be
        ...how to be a different me...

evolve. revolve.

looser now, not tighter
world don't need another fighter
heartfelt, bone-felt,
either way...
            not shutting down,
                    just turn around

look deeper now

find home in me
make home in me
be home, in me

whole body castle

not finger, arm, shoulder,
        or knee,
                but every little part of me
                        hold every part now, tenderly

growing me
let-go-ing me
not giving up the space in me
not the way to set me free...

new breath in and old breath out
heart sheds slowly, layered doubt

thanking you for helping me...
just thanking you for helping me.

INNER UNRAVEL

Staying present in this body
isn't one of my favorite past-times.
Not-so-funny thing is,
I had no idea how long I'd been checking out of it.

Left alone,
old familiar company
moves in, surrounding me.

Seeking to interest me
in fascinating sensations
that I am
trying not to
disappear into.

Some voice inside me tells me to calm down,
to settle, to let the fire burn out
or at least simmer to a rage.

Another voice from all around
recommends a different route – this one I am drawn to.

"How can you know it if you don't live it?
Get in there. Just go on..."

And so, I go.

For my life so far, I've been "going,"
many times without even
stopping to know it.

I don't wait around for chatter,
or for someone else to go first,
or for all the talk about what might or might not happen.

Something about me doesn't care to sit through it.

...and so, I just go.

To this day, I wonder why I've never been
as afraid as "I should have been."

To this day, my sole concern was not once for me.

Like I didn't really exist.
Like I never really did.

I went along like nothing was happening
to or even around me
    'cuz in a way, I guess it wasn't.

Seems I'd rather separate
even when some have told me not to.

Staying present in this body
isn't one of my favorite past-times.

Not-so-funny thing is,
I had no idea how long I'd been checking out of it.

It's an interesting catch because I love life.
Being in love with it, opens me to this
present-time heartbreak I guess.

I believe there is some understanding coming.

Not from the outside – I don't worry about that...

        it's what's unraveling in here
            that has my soul attention today.

JARRED EMOTION

jars of carefully placed emotion
sealed so tightly, no commotion
not strong enough to break them open

until today

moving toward the source of me
touching now, the things I see

jars of carefully placed emotion
sealed so tightly, no commotion
not strong enough to break them open

until today

each jar holds a folded story
tucked in with the birth it gave

I view from here, through the
glass of the jar

they talk to me
while I hear god

which voice goes to who?

crashing open,
shards of glass,
tearing at the walls of me,
eating at the strength of me

I'm so tired.

Asking what I feel now.

Dead tired.
Unrelenting exhaustion.

...did I mention tired?

so, thank you for letting me rest here,
with you,
with me.

infant warrior,
done in.

taking off every possible shield,
putting down every sword,
lying down all defense ever known to me.

EVER known to me.

I want…just…to hold onto you…

in this moment where I am

perfectly raw.

I know you see this in me.
I trust you see this in me.
I trust your care.

Thank you for your care.

somebody said, "I felt that way once too."

I know it's meant to help,
but how much should I give to them,
for their experience of this "feeling"?

Whose is it?

Mine? Yours? Theirs?
Who wants it?
Free to the taker...

that's the joke.

Knowing how it feels,
I take it in before the taste
makes another mouth bitter.

Easy thing
is to kill the other.
I prefer to take that
challenge to myself.

To not kill you,
parts of me will die.

What have I done?
        Who am I before you now?
            How have I done this?

You refuse to see
damage done.
Your wisdom.
I so love you for this.

We will grow.

Today.
Tomorrow.
        Forever.

No death has to happen here.
It already has.

Behind us now,
in the halls of mirrors
where vision is clear.

A man walks past
on the street,
winks at me.
Some would say
he wants to take me to bed.
Maybe he thinks so, too.

Imagination runs.
Maybe he recognizes me
from 4,000 years ago,
where we formed a fire together
at the foot of a dear master's bed
                              as he died.
We bonded in that death.

In this life,
he is a stranger
who walks past me on the
street, and winks.

How far have we grown apart?

Is it good or bad that this
memory lives in only some
of us today?

Today...as if it is real.

Why is this book open to me?
Legible?

Alone becomes a way.

Still, there is one who would speak
to my every dimension.

One who would
allow me to set down
the weapons I've been
carrying for so, so long now.

Who would have the courage
to meet me here,
everywhere,
and love me here,
everywhere.

More than my mother?

We *are* the mother.

Together – tunnels of
        inner vision make way to one another.

Program is simply complicated.

Find each other,
        be free,
                know LOVE.

LANDED

*Today, I am moving in
from the inside out.*

Today, I am moving in
from the inside out.

Looked okay from out there,
but now, from inside here
                    there's work to do.

The ones who invite me
to go and play for a while -
"a while" there is much different
than what this form expects.

In the "while" - much happens.

Connections are not properly made.

Foundation is not steady.

Flexible? Oh yes...

This form picks things up
        that do not belong to it,
                    or even with it.

It needs to be
carefully maintained.

"I" need to be carefully maintained ~
                    handled with my own care.

Some have said that
what I have is a blessing.
I'm not always sure I agree.

I'm not sorry for it,
but at the same time,
I'm not quick to wish this memory
and this way of living on another.

Being peaceful is a blessing.
Enjoying sunshine is a blessing.
Knowing love is a blessing.

To remember where I've come from,
     how I've formed,
         what I'm about,

     why I chose this...

       where some God is....

Blessing?
Maybe.

But sometimes

     it does nothing more

       than hurt

         a whole lot.

The closeness is so close that the
distance is deadly.

There are limitations here.
I have to remember *THAT*.

I am no longer the rainbow,
    yet it is with me.

I am not the earth,
    yet she owns me.

I am not the stars,
    yet they share me.

I am on *this* planet,

    in *this* body,

      with *this* blessing,

        in *this* life.

Anyway, I am only love.

I want to line up,
in the light,
in *this* love,
    with you.

What you say to me

    sometimes connects

      like a waterfall

        tumbling down and through...

When I am just right with you
(though I've never known a
wrong with you),

when we are "just so"....

I know the greatest joy possible

as every connection

connects.

This peace and *this* love and *this* joy...inimitable.

Every sense connects. Every sense, finds light.

We are a circle

among circles

within circles.

When I get here, I am alive and well.

I don't have time to miss out on this anymore.

I want to find this place as often as possible,

forever would be best.

"Landed," you said.

...perhaps I have finally *landed*.

LIFE'S BATH WATER

feel it as it happens here
it can't be touched by you
from there
honor when your heart is dying
feel it when your eyes are crying

running life like bath water
watching, touching with a fingertip
pulled back by cold
drawn in by heat

measuring, just so

until my body can rest in warmth

is this not the journey I am on?

until my body can rest in warmth
until I *know* my body is resting in warmth

is this not the journey I am on?

out there, I know so well
from behind eyes that were silent,
not fear.

....sorrow? Closer to truth.

I've known so many forms
before this one
touched stars, held them in my pockets
of space...

vibrations through and through
and through to God

no eyes to melt there
no fingers to ache there
no heart to break there
no love to miss there

a baby thought the difference was
to love them all
warrior on one side true
born to life too small to move

no breath, no voice, no cry, no choice

watching God from every angle
meet me, love me, see me, kill me
it's all in God, that's what I hear
but this little body met such fear

hands around me,
blades upon me,
death within me
meet your father

I watch them cry
with bone dry eyes
little baby, watch emotion
take it in, it's real, it's real

real like what?
like the galaxy that dropped me here?
like God, you say that I must fear?
like the ship that took me home last night?
explode, implode, it's all alright...

he couldn't help the things he'd done
I don't hate him,
lesson one

I hated me for living through
to see the damage I would do
later life would call to me
to do my part to set him free
if any thought goes out to him
let it be for peace within
his tired heart, his heavy heart
love him, love him
that's my part

crumpled baby, no more tears
put away her daddy's fears
ate them all up
one by one,
smiling, dying,
there, all done...

not so bad,
not even sad...who said it wouldn't be easy?

God says this is not
his intention
that I am more than
some invention
not his plan for me this time
to be the one to pantomime
some way through life
some way through hell

I've done it all so very well
but now that's in the past of me
a way I can no longer be
if life this time shall set me free...

free.

a feeling? no.
a dream? not hardly.
a truth? much warmer.
me? you're on.

feel it as it happens here
it can't be touched by you
from there
honor when your heart is dying
feel it when your eyes are crying
your body will support your mission
all you have to do is listen...

let it tell you all it knows
from your beautiful crown
to the earth of your toes

feel it, taste it, touch it, own it
only for a moment now
let it move on past you now
listen to him guide you now

find the closest friend
I've known
in years and lives and journeys home
to far within and deep with-out
the journey's what it's all about...

Really? I ask, really so?
who can say the way to go?
who can say what's here to know?
who can help me? Where'd they go?

Angels, angels meet me here,
take away this baby's fear
of meeting this thick atmosphere
knowing fully that one tear
could tear apart a mother's heart...

What good is that? What good am I?

I ask and ask

I do not cry
the tears that run the walls of me
the pain that often talks of me
that clings to me and eats at me
it never, ever sets me free...

feel the warmth of energy
touching every part
of me

take it in,
it's real, it's real...

LOVE YOU LIKE THAT

Did you feel that vibration?
That was my quake -
kind of a bold declaration to make.

Did you feel that vibration?
    That was my quake -
        kind of a bold declaration to make.

Doesn't always last long,
sure I'll take you along,
    to a place not yet tried
        promise you won't misinterpret the ride.

Don't love me like that.
Love you like that.

That partnership will last
    a whole lot longer than
what you can imagine here

Let me warn you of
one   other   thing

I'm kind of a reckless driver.

You might want to take your own wheel.
I would fully advise it,
        if you're up for advice….

great ride though.

If you catch these just right,
    the world explodes into truth.

Becomes much too much to let go.

So yeah, take your own wheel…
        love you like that.

MOTHER OF MOTHERS

Had a vision of our Mother of mothers.

She was crying.

Had a vision of our Mother of mothers.

She was crying.

In one tear,
one single tear,

was our entire world and with it

our universe.

Still, with room to spare.

...Are those *my* tears too...?

She says they cannot be. I must learn my own.
She watched the day that mine were stolen.
Says they are still wearing my name...

All of this, in her
One
    Single
        Tear.

Hands to her chest.

Love.

...and I think *my* heart breaks...

I know nothing of compassion.

MY VOICE

Who is talking to you now?
Whose voice fills your ears today?

Who is talking to you now?
Whose voice fills your ears today?

Surprise...today, it is my own.

I am hearing now, that today,
    more than ever,

I have got to hear and
honor the voice within me
that says,

"Everything is okay.
All clear, all clear, all clear."

My voice, has got to be

louder,
    bigger,
        stronger

than any other
that I hear speak of me.

I have to believe in me, for me,
just as I believe in you, for you.

Perhaps I've never loved
as honestly as I today love you.

For this thought to you, I will grow two.

                One stays home with me.

SAFE HAVEN

to feel my heart break
without a smile on my face

foreign to me

to know that I
     have a place
          where anything
               can go

how can I ever
     thank you for this?

established trust

feeling,
     beyond any words

you hold my tears
     with a sacred hand

to feel them against my skin
is foreign to me

to feel my heart break
without a smile on my face

foreign to me

going all the way back
to the baby I was

          baby I am

baby blanket comfort here

fearful heart goes fearless here

          tender safe haven, rattling soul.

SAMURAI

tiny child
fingers' reach
instead of a doll
she pulled in
a sword

and here are the presents
she left behind

not knowing they were hers

tiny child
fingers' reach
instead of a doll
she pulled in
a sword

grown today
for whatever
that means

baby inside
reaches for the
soft
plush of the
teddy bear heart

he hands it to her
with love
in his reach

it has been
here for you
for all time

blade by her
samurai side,
others in her grip

no fingers free to
touch the soft –

  taken in only
   by eyes

reaching, he says
it's for her,
the baby there
that died...

laying down the
weapon now –
just one, not all just yet

one hand
she holds
the teddy bear,

heart becomes
their own

     the other
     holds the blade...

SCARED TO LIFE

I sat alone the other day,
searching for that place in the space
between my life and some death.

There was some breakdown.
Something got too close.

I sat alone the other day,

   searching for that place in the space

      between my life and some death.

By the time I got there it was full.
Not with people, places, things or names,
but filled with lines, and noise and sounds.

I don't know what that was or is.
Can't remember having been there before.

I got to thinking,
before this wall was kicked in,

I was really something wasn't I?

Somebody said to me the other day,
"You just don't seem like yourself."

I wanted to ask who that would be.

Who *was* I? Could someone remind me?
I just can't seem to remember anymore...

You asked me if I was still afraid.

No. Just tired.

There is a reason I was looking at the wall
when I answered,
                    you knew that already.

….but, it was kinda true I guess…

I'm not afraid.

PETRIFIED is here,
dancing along my skin.

…and I truly am tired.

Tired of being scared to life.

My back is to the wall. I don't like it here.
I am not inside or outside of me.
I don't know who I am.

The outside of me is someone
the world around me built –
the seemingly confident,
pliable, strong
outer flesh side of me.

Almost bought into the story myself,
now learning that it
doesn't match the
inside so well.

As I write this,
my heart is burning in my chest.
My fingers do not want to cooperate,
they seem to hate this activity.

Eyes are running, filling with tears
laced with something that
does not let them fall.

Thoughts, scrambling.

...and I *am* afraid.

every   single   day

have been for as long as I can remember.

OF WHAT?

            ...Of What?

                        ...of what...?

tiny, whispered,
barely audible response,
echoes in an old,
        trying-to-be-forgotten
                    chamber.

Within that haunted buried space,
remains this toxic, time-worn
memory of a
        failing
            falling
                broken
                    human
                    being.

"I am afraid" goes something like this...

I am afraid of not being able to make anyone
proud of me, not even for one flash of any second.

I am afraid of not being able to make a
difference in one single life.

I am afraid that I will fail in all that I do.
I am afraid I am not good at anything.

I am afraid that I will be a disappointment
to the handful of precious teachers
who have come
to help me.

I don't know why they have come,
I don't know why I am so fortunate –
but I am afraid they will catch on
and realize that I am not worth their
gifted time or effort.

I am afraid that their time and attention will be wasted on
me, to have received these treasures and to fail to make
something good come of it...

I am afraid that they wouldn't have expected any other
outcome.

I am afraid nobody believes in me.
I am afraid that I don't blame them.

I have never been satisfied with my _any_ performance.
Never.

I am convinced that people are humoring me
when they say I have done something well...

I am afraid I get the joke.

When I hear, "I love you,"
I wonder who that person is talking to.

I am afraid that this one afraid

    Might

            Never

                    Hear

                            "I love you."

SOME TRUTH APPEARED

Hearing voices not in my ears, but in my body –
from some other place,
mixed with tones that make my brain ache
and blood tremble.

So what is it? Come close or go away?

Is there somewhere in between?

Does it belong to all of us, together?

I think this is where we all started
not that long ago.

Now we have forgotten.

Now we have inane hoops to jump through
just to connect once again.

How silly is this?

Anyhow, I thought I was doing much better,
but then some truth appeared.

Not doing so great.
Some might even call it lousy.
Discombobulated.
It's getting old. And frustrating.
Just like me.

My chest is making me sick. I don't feel good at all.

I've taken a turn for somewhere ugly and I don't want to

go
    one
        more
            step.

Frozen, right here.
If I talk about it I have to open my mouth.
If I open my mouth, I'm thinkin' I might puke.

Nearing my stomach and chest now,

I can't breathe.

    ...so, time to release it.

Release it?!
Hell, I don't even want to touch it...

Hearing voices not in my ears, but in my body —
    from some other place,
mixed with tones that make my brain ache
and blood tremble.

It is absolutely pitch black where I am right now.
My head feels like it's being clenched in a vise and
there is a thickness all around me that I can
barely push my body through.

I don't want to move.

I am afraid of what is surrounding me.

I feel that if I move,
I will die another hundred and four violent deaths.

I want to just be quiet...
        really, really quiet.

I don't even want to breathe.
Backing up in search of a wormhole
that will swallow me whole.

Help me to disappear.

Can't back up.

There's a wall behind me, in this noisy, black place.
I stick to it like mud.
I wish I could be more like super glue,
but the sweat on my spine
has made me slippery.

I hate it here.

I am very afraid and very, very alone.

"All" is leaving me here alone to die now,
but this is different from the ones I've known before.

I am horrified.

Since when is death scary to me?

So.

There's no way out.

...I think I'm going to have to close the distance I know I
am putting between myself and those who are trying to
love me...including me...

Somehow, I understand that every
painful,
        miserable

            step
                of
                    this

is very necessary.

Beyond this,
there is a peace I know.
Waiting to be claimed.
By me.

Yes, I am sure of that.

It sits, holding my place in this world...
                        calling me by name.
Not the calling we hear with ears,
                but the kind that calls to *cells*.

Dancing.
Longing.

                A C H I N G.

Forget it.
I'm running the other way.
And I mean, *hauling* back the other way.

There is no fast to describe this fast.

No, I don't want to be here today after all.
Maybe I wasn't looking so forward to this finding.

I wonder where I'm going.

I am so lost that it begins to piss me off.

Deciding to be done,
I feel my heart grow hard within my chest.

My inside begins to freeze.
I feel it, and I know it.

I don't care.

I lay there, closing,
        closing,
closing
every door,
every window,
every hole,
every nook,
every cranny.

Lock down.

I am really, really, really pissed off.

I tell myself that it must be that
I have come to the end of this pursuit
of the reconnecting of this
severed relationship within me.

Must be time for me to move on.

And with that I know in my heart,

   ....what a mighty coward I am.

Something has broken me wide open.

I am struggling.
This is the hardest, ugliest fight of my life.

Yet I realize,
it IS a fight for my very life.

This "something" that started it all,

I hate it.

But more than that, I love it.

 So isn't this what's going on?

Death isn't such a stranger to me.

Life is.

I think I came in backwards.

WOULD GO

I would go where none have gone before
would throw my heart out on the floor
would gladly meet your demons first
would give my water for your thirst

I would run through darkness to bring you light,
would give my eyes to offer sight,
I would walk through flames that know no end,
would turn around and go again

but what about for me?

I would go where none have gone before
would throw my heart out on the floor
would gladly meet your demons first
would give my water for your thirst

but what about for me?

I would rise to greet you every day
would offer love along your way
would give you all I have to give
would surely die to let you live

but what about for me?

some sadness weighs upon me
like a cloak of heavy weight
some worry wraps around me
like some unrelenting fate

the light of john says,
"go there, tell me what you see"
so I venture off, uncertain

on a quest in search of me

I would give you running mountain streams
would give you all my best of dreams
would take your fears and call them mine
would stand with you throughout all time

but what about for me?

I would face your monsters one by one
would give to you my morning sun
would jump across and build a bridge
would help you safely off the edge

but what about for me?

some loneliness demanding
full attention in some way
uncertainty alive and well
goes with me through my day

the light of john says,
"leave it, it wasn't yours to take"
so I drop it where I stand right now

and with it, goes the ache

I would shelter you from wind and rain
would take from you your strongest pain
would give my strength and all my might
to protect you through your longest night

but what about for me?

I would give to you my favorite things
and every joy your heart can sing
would take your hand when others won't
would break your fall if others don't

but what about for me?

If I do not love myself like this,
then I cannot fully love
If I do not take control of me
forever will be the search of
the vision or the driver
or the lighter or the way,

instead, the light of john asks,

"who's 'in control' today?"

I'm 'kind of in control' of me,
am worth the love I give.
I'll try not to take for granted,
that it's love which makes us live.

With what I have to offer,
with what I have to share,

I must include my Self with others,

so love lives everywhere.

TESTS ENDED

The day you were born,
all tests ended.

what I heard today.

The day you were born,
all tests ended.

Whatever you
have experienced
after that...

well, that's been
                your call.

Do not miss the
true miracle of your body.

You manifested it.

Appreciate it.
Appreciate and love it.

The things you notice
along your way,

that which you so love
and enjoy
and appreciate

do not forget to
begin right there,

        with you.

UNIVERSAL TEACHING

Universal teaching,
offered on the wind.

Universal teaching,
        offered on the wind.

"You didn't see it the first time
because your mind didn't allow it.
Not open."

Me.   I won't argue with that.

Breeze rustles auburn, damp
        leaves to the earth
                we share.

"It isn't brought to you, to argue.
Nothing is.
It is brought to you,
to experience the *all* of it.

Most of all,
brought to you
for the developing taste of
your very human experience."

Me.   Taste?

seems
forever
bittersweet...

WHAT YOU SEE

And, your initials are already carved here,
on my heart. See?

I want to learn to be that tree.

I'm going to

    Need
        Your
            help,

for however long it takes.

      ...can you do this for me?

           ....with me?

Well, I can promise this in return.

When I am that tree,
I might make you very proud.

And, your initials are already carved here,
          on my heart. See?

So what do you say?

....please. help me to see
       What you see in me....

JACKET

The elbows are torn,
belt somewhat tattered,
but it still holds its own
and I guess that's what matters.

This jacket's beginning to fit a bit better.
It's pretty comfy in all kinds of weather.

The elbows are torn,
        belt somewhat tattered,
            but it still holds its own
                        and I guess that's what matters.

I think of the times
        I have tried to disown it,
            remember the times
        I have kicked it and thrown it.

Left it in places
I've not ventured back to,
gave it to strangers
who seemed to want two...

                Funny thing though -
                    it's still on my back - see?

No matter what I did....

                        it didn't desert me.

I'M FINE

My eyes are exhausted of these
side images and shadows
that never seem to leave me alone anymore.

Feeling somewhat better today.

The back of my head is wilting away
like a flower with no water,
becoming intense
with fierce burning,

sometimes ripping apart
at what I'm sure are the seams...

Other than that, I'm fine.

My neck has become a tightrope,
taught with cables and currents and dreams,
it is holding my head on,
though barely letting me breathe -
doesn't seem to believe
I need the air anymore...

My shoulders are aching, not cooperating,
reminding me that I'm human
and that they are too,
as my remaining joints are screaming
with rust.

Though I use them regularly, they feel neglected...

Other than that, I'm fine.

My eyes are exhausted of these
side images and shadows
that never seem to leave me alone anymore.

There is always some movement,
some brush, some streak,
some color, some warping,
some cloudiness,
some sleeplessness.

They just keep absorbing and watching and feeding
this mind of mine
that simply won't
settle
down.

My ears are supportive of my eyes' new purpose,
which seems to be bombarding me with
loudness and movement and crashing
and thrashing and warp speeds and no speed,

they change in mid-sentence,
but they're helping me become
quite the actress…sure, I hear you just fine….

if I only knew what language you were speaking
I'm sure I could have quite the conversation with you.

And if I could comprehend one full sentence today,

I'm sure that whatever it is you're saying
is really very interesting,

but there's some sort of meltdown happening
with my communication abilities today –

would it be rude of me to ask if maybe you could come
back and try again tomorrow…?

Otherwise, really, I'm fine.

My hands are dropping things,
literally ungrabbing things,
out of unison with what I think I'm doing.

Fingers aren't typing, they are just pushing…
like no memory has ever been given to them
and no years of typing ever existed
across them.

They are ignoring me it seems.

My chest?   I won't talk about.
My heart?   That neither.
My center?   Can't feel it.
My breath?   Can't breathe it.

…and so…this is the battle I'm waging inside me…

There is heat and cold racing around me,
my palms are so hot I can't stand them,
yet sometimes so cold I think surely I've died.

But I'm sure once I sleep again this will all be better…

in the meantime,
no problem – I'm fine.

DEATH HAD A BOUNTY

The voice of your eyes
told me that you
could escort me through
death
and back.

Only right now,
this many years after our first meeting

>   do I even begin to
>   understand

the impact of

you

in my life.

You showed me truth.

The voice of your eyes

told me that you

could escort me through

death

and back.

Could.
But would not.

Warrior.

Death had a bounty on me before you.

THROUGHOUT MY FALLING

there is a calling
throughout my falling
that tells me of past times
when I used to make rhymes
with words not yet spoken
full chains never broken

there is a calling
throughout my falling
that tells me of past times
when I used to make rhymes
with words not yet spoken
full chains never broken
and still they circle our universe
calling out continuous
connecting me to me to me
to all the things my eyes now see
to you and you and you and you
and all the things we'll someday do
and there is love behind this connection
that began in the orbit of what some call heaven

but god is laughing because
he says we're reaching
so far for his teaching
instead of looking everywhere
even in the rat's ass hair
where sacred is as sacred does
and god says it's the way to us
to where we know the truth of truth
to where we know the youth of youth

mostly I am dancing here
jumping from this place of fear
where I am forgetting
that I have been betting
on love to make our world the place
on love to help us end the race
of winning first, of dying first
of giving all to die of thirst

it isn't what he wants for us
he wonders what we did with trust
that brought us here to live again
he brings us to him once again

the meeting of angels
who've fallen in tangles
and wipes the blood from our
battle-zone faces,
and reminds us again of our beautiful places
where we born truth and love and light
he's asking us to put down the fight
to trust that he will do what's right
and he is the one who has sent us back here
and we were the ones who promised
without fear

but here we are, clinging to past-times
when we were the warriors making the lines
for heaven to come forward again
facing every demon then
and when we see the glimpse of darkness
we become the wrath of starkness
quick to draw our blades to strike
those who don't deserve the light

but god says he is watching it
we're in the middle of his favorite shit
it's a promise we have made to him
before he sent us back again
see, on the other side of living
you and I were short of giving
people here didn't feel our reach
we tried to speak but could not teach

from the other side of heaven's walls
so we agreed to take the fall

and god sent us back with memory
of these things now we taste and see
and when the darkness takes us under
and when we stop and trip and wonder
he says from the inside out,
"It's all the light, that's what we're about."

he says if there's something other than love
it isn't what we're really made of,
the essence of living
is what he is giving
and what we create then
is in our own hands then
and the blackness we see
is made by man
confused by what he thinks he can
change in our world,
from the outside in
but we know this is not where to begin

and god is looking upon his fleet
of warriors who have died at his feet
raising us up now
to teach us to learn how
to become the light he shared with us
to send us back to teach of love
and those who come to you and I
are those who will be unafraid to die
because we've done it so many times
they will be free to live this time

and this is the training that comes our way
it isn't what we know of today...

we've been trained for a spiritual war
that's always been at some heaven's door
but to understand the feelings of those who have suffered
we agreed to this, back when we were tougher
but now as it comes, we falter inside
you and I have nowhere to hide
because the truth eats away at our exhausted souls
and we suffer in silence as nobody knows
that what we live for is what we have died for
and just when we think we can't possibly take more

god reminds me that we have a deal
and he is there, helping us heal

in every way, in every part
truth is here in our own beating hearts

and he is watching as we grow up now
he says he has never been more proud
of his warriors' graces, wiping blood from their faces

and he says we should keep right on now
and he will continue to show us how
to reach within to find our place
and he will help to guide our pace
and when we question the core of truth here
this is when we are most near
the goal of our true learning
the reasoning for our returning
to be the warriors this god has trained
keeping us in freezing rain

pushing us through fires of hell
leaving us with no story to tell
but bringing us much closer in,
remembering what we promised then...

do not give up, do not let go
do not close off to the truth we know

It's all about the truth my friend
for us, this truth shall never end.

PEACEMAKER

*You are angry with yourself for
giving in to being born.*

been working with Buddha

You have red pouring from
your pores.

What has caused you such anger?

You forgot to include yourself.

Responsibility is yours.

You are angry with yourself for
giving in to being born.

You are so in love with life
yet you are hating yourself for this love.

You are not afraid of anything
except of being found out
how lovely you are.

You are awesome.

Let go of all that you have taken and killed.

You have been given another chance,
exactly as you are.

It is not and never has been
your job to take this on.

IT IS NOT BEING GIVEN TO YOU.

What is being given to you?

Freedom from remorse?

Would you take that
as easily as you
take in sorrow?

I would advise it.

Live awake or asleep.

You are a peacemaker
with or without your
"doing."

It's who you are before you
returned to the world.

Inside, inside, inside...
you know who you are.

Nothing in your life has been
without reason.

Nothing.

Structure is to make trouble.
Learn to live with it.

Problem-solver.

Make problems if you don't have them.
Make them manageable.

How committed are you?

    Here, to this "self" you have.

Not harder. Softer.

You only have two arms
this time.

Others are on loan
to you in the instant
of your request.

Your request comes so often,
you believe these arms to be yours
in your current human body.

Pay better attention to your current human body.

This is how a walk to peace is somewhat understood.

Just

       start

           walking.

LOAN ME YOUR EYES

Loan me your eyes honey,
clue me in on what you see,
I'm afraid I don't quite see it
on the other side of me.

Loan me your eyes honey,
clue me in on what you see,

I'm afraid I don't quite see it
on the other side of me.

You show me something awesome,
in which I can believe,

you shine on me with all that light,
seems never on reprieve.

Even when I'm running
out on me and who I am,

you plant yourself right next to me,
you do not leave your stand.

You show me a security

with love
            you
                    circle
            back
        to me.

Loan me your eyes honey,
show me what I do –
help me see the way I look
on the other side of you.

Loan me your eyes honey,
show me who I am,
the way I look to you from there,
please help me if you can.

Loan me your eyes honey,
show me what you see,
what I wouldn't give to have
the faith your eyes shine back to me.

Loan me your ears honey,
so I can hear the words I say,

Loan me some of who you are honey,

help me make it through today.

LACK OF BOUNDARY

Confucius tells me to
mind my place
and that by doing so
I will understand
my worth

familiar crowd

since this atmosphere
speaks of my
selfishness

lack of gratitude

even beyond my
own lack of boundary

capable body
(on a good day)

able mind
to this I could laugh

I do laugh

they frown

selfish again,
as I continue to smile
they call it
rude

I wonder who's ruder

Confucius tells me to
mind my place
and that by doing so
I will understand
my worth

maybe I'd mind it
if I could find it

Lao Tsu
suggests
that it's all one place
one universal space

I can't quite buy
this anymore
as languages pour in
from every pore

and there are many
not just one million

I can't see just one
can't feel just one
can't taste just one

cover my ears,
eyes, nose,
throat
to their sound
knowing
the ride
will be a long one

they invite
me out of
this cellular frame

gaining the memory
that cannot

so comfortably return

why can't I
comfortably return?

fit isn't right
line-up not so easy

should have stayed put
the first billion times

re-placing my self
just outside of
all
reach

makes me feel
like a cheater
somehow

some anger
licking my fingertips

some fear
tapping on
my eyelids

some sadness
beating
on my heart

outside heart

pain so great
all I can do
is smile

who says it's not
so great?

I would disagree.

pain is great

can make one smile for
day-long-lifetimes

talking with the
angel

losing interest

not afraid to die again.

angel whispered,

"It's the return.

It's always your return

that's
never
once
been
easy."

NOT ALONE

When someone meets your eyes for the first time
with absolute fear, not of who you are,
but fear of no longer knowing who you are,
it will do something to your soul.

In those moments when the world stands still,
and when you feel like you are most alone,
I would like for you to know that you are only so
if you need to be, prefer to be, choose to be.

I am always here for you,
in every shape -
to lean on, to hold on, to blow in the breeze with,
to fall apart with.

I do not claim to have any answer,
any secret, any plan.

But I do have the courage to stand with you
when you are facing the ugliest ugly,
loneliest lonely, most terrifying unexplainable stuff
the universe lays out for you along this path.

When someone meets your eyes for the first time
with absolute fear, not of who you are,
but fear of no longer knowing who you are,
it will do something to your soul.

I do not know what that is.

If the eyes that are meeting yours
happen to be in the mirror,
trust that you are on your way.

Know that you are GOOD inside,
and no matter the battles that begin to wage,
know that you are strong.

There are times when "being in control" becomes
a really interesting way to kill yourself.

Some things are beyond control.
Some things only require "attention,"
    otherwise, they will teach you of "control."

trust me when I say it is not what we know of
in this world.

When you are smiling on the outside
and dying on the inside,
when you are standing tall but are unable to move,
when you are overwhelmed by grief and heartbreak and
not one instant of peace can be found...

if you can make your way to only one thought,
let it be this.

You are not alone.

I am right there,
wherever you are,
wherever you are...

hugging you, if you need it,
encouraging you, if you need it,
sitting by you, if you need it,
helping you up, if you need it,
tasting your rage, if you need it,
living your hell, if you need it.

Someone once told me,

"It's okay to not have the answers.
Sometimes, you need something more than that.
That something, would be love."

I'm not sure I really tasted that until now.

But here, where there are no answers,
it begins to make some kind of sense.

SOFTLY

    hearing

        UNIVERSAL VOICE

      echoing

        forever

      I AM here for you.

ABOUT THE AUTHOR

Author of *healing happens*, Michelle grew up in Chicago, the youngest of 7 and fortunate enough to be raised by one who encouraged exploration and growth in all directions. At a young age, she began writing, influenced by things around her, both visible and non-visible.

Treasured experiences built an interest in the exploration of life and spirit energy through many avenues. These studies and pursuits continue through her practice of Aikido and Traditional Chinese Medicine.

Michelle is a licensed acupuncturist and co-founder of Acupuncture & Oriental Medicine as well as an instructor of Aikido at the Abiding Spirit Center and the Aikido Shimboku Kai.

She openly invites conversation and feedback about any of her writings. Please take the time to visit her Facebook author page – Michelle L. Tate and share your thoughts.

15956995R00078

Made in the USA
Charleston, SC
28 November 2012